For Roland,

who has kept the

Jared

Les Barricades Mystérieuses

This is copy 23 of one hundred first editions especially numbered and signed for release on Sunday 25 April 1999

by

Jared Carter

Jared Carter

Les Barricades Mystérieuses

Thirty-Two Villanelles

Cleveland State University
Poetry Center

Copyright © 1987, 1991, 1992, 1993, 1994, 1995, 1996, 1997, 1998, and 1999 by Jared Carter. All rights reserved.

Edward Calvert's "Chamber Idyll" on the front cover is copyright © by the British Museum and reproduced by permission. The illustrations on pages ix, 9, 19, and 29 and on the back cover are copyright © by Dover Publications and reproduced by permission.

"Improvisation," "Linen," and "Hawkmoth" first appeared in *Poetry* and are copyright © 1987, 1994, and 1995 by the Modern Poetry Association. "Improvisation" was included in *A Lent Sourcebook: The Forty Days*, published in 1990 by Liturgy Training Publications, an imprint of the Archdiocese of Chicago. Additional acknowledgments appear on page 45.

Thanks to John Robertson, Bradley Omanson, Jean Lunn, J. Kates, David Evett, Lenny Emmanuel, Jim Cory, Selene Carter, R. P. Burnham, and William Baer and the staff of *The Formalist*. Special thanks to Leonard Trawick, of the Cleveland State University Poetry Center, who edited and produced this book and three of the author's previous books. *Ave atque vale!*

Library of Congress Catalog Card Number: 98-72252

Manufactured in the United States of America

ISBN 1-880834-40-5

First printing 1999

Contents

Improvisation	1
Dusk	2
Summons	3
Riverdrift	4
Candle	5
Encore	6
Berceuse	7
Solstice	8
Bridge	11
Ditchweed	12
Cemetery	13
Buzzards	14
Portage	15
Plantain	16
Interlude	17
Ford	18
Millefiori	21
Clavichord	22
Waterspout	23
Loess	24
Parfumeur	25
Mandragora	26
Tankroom	27
Phosphorescence	28
Palimpsest	31
Labyrinth	32
Raincrow	33
Linen	34
Sortilege	35
Reprise	36
Hawkmoth	37
Comet	38
Notes	41
Acknowledgments	45

for Diane

Purity of heart is to will one thing

He who does not imagine in stronger and better lineaments, and in stronger and better light than his perishing and mortal eye can see, does not imagine at all.

William Blake

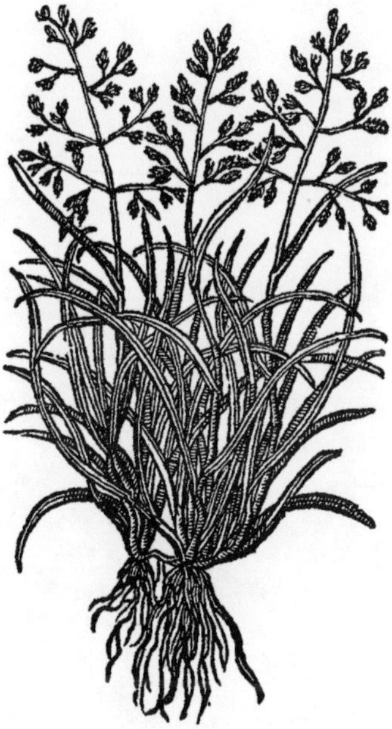

Improvisation

To improvise, first let your fingers stray
across the keys like travelers in snow:
each time you start, expect to lose your way.

You'll find no staff to lean on, none to play
among the drifts the wind has left in rows.
To improvise, first let your fingers stray

beyond the path. Give up the need to say
which way is right, or what the dark stones show;
each time you start, expect to lose your way.

And what the stillness keeps, do not betray;
the one who listens is the one who knows.
To improvise, first let your fingers stray;

out over emptiness is where things weigh
the least. Go there, believe a current flows
each time you start: expect to lose your way.

Risk is the pilgrimage that cannot stay;
the keys grow silent in their smooth repose.
To improvise, first let your fingers stray.
Each time you start, expect to lose your way.

Dusk

This gleaming—sleek light through the window,
caught by the hall mirror—lingering, lost,
vanishing into pattern over fresh snow,

coruscating for a moment where windrows
slant, where junipers stand bleak with frost.
This gleaming, sleek light through the window,

strangely undulant, able to quicken, show
fencerow or stump, pile of stones embossed,
vanishing into pattern. Over fresh snow,

a last few flakes drift through shadow,
quiescent now, no longer spreading across
this gleaming. Sleek light through the window:

a match struck. The flare, the gradual glow
of the lamp's wick, the chimney's pale gloss,
vanishing into pattern. Over fresh snow,

outside, no light remains. Within, the slow
adjustment to evening—this soft pentecost,
this gleaming. Sleek light through the window,
vanishing into pattern, over fresh snow.

Summons

A log shifts, sending a few sparks higher.
Outside, through the larches, an owl calls.
The dog's asleep. On the hearth near the fire,

carefully stacked, in a basket of woven wire,
wood for the night. A stick of kindling falls,
a log shifts, sending a few sparks higher,

changing the shadows in the room. A spire
of light glints on the clock's face in the hall.
The dog's asleep. On the hearth, near the fire,

he begins to whine, to become a far crier
among the hills, twitching his feathered paws.
A log shifts, sending a few sparks higher;

his ears prick: ahead, some stark desire
steps forth, waiting to hold him in thrall.
The dog's asleep on the hearth, near the fire;

he is farther away now, part of a choir
of lost voices. He falls back, sprawls.
A log shifts, sending a few sparks higher;
the dog's asleep on the hearth near the fire.

Riverdrift

They come to life again—freshwater pearls
tumbling and turning in a salt-glazed bowl.
Catching the light within the random swirls

we stir among them, patterned by the whorls
of our fingertips, brightening as they roll,
they come to life again. Freshwater pearls—

culls, not worth keeping—saved by some girl
or grandmother, years ago. A last shoal,
catching the light within the random swirls

of the lantern's glow, or the shifting world
of shadows cast by the fire. Lustrous, whole,
they come to life again. Freshwater pearls

that take on a part of us now, from the whirls
of our touch—shapes on a screen, or scroll,
catching the light within. The random swirls,

the liquid sounds, the way the river skirls
into sudden spray, or sun-struck aureole
they come to life again, freshwater pearls
catching the light within the random swirls.

Candle

It is your naked body now I see,
released from all restraint, once more revealed
among the shadows, where you wait to be.

What incorporeal fire, what lambency
could be as bright? Brilliant and unconcealed,
it is your naked body now I see,

where facing mirrors gleam. That transiency—
the deepening of your image there—will yield,
among the shadows where you wait to be,

a nether self—a rising on the sea,
a wind that moves across an open field.
It is your naked body now I see

approaching, yet projected endlessly
away from me, by some enchantment sealed
among the shadows. Where you wait to be,

the parallels converge, the mystery
remains: what comes together is the real.
It is your naked body now I see
among the shadows where you wait to be.

Encore

At times, perhaps, along the empty halls
that once led past so many different doors,
linking the silences within these walls,

they seem to stir—not to reach out, or call,
more like a whispering across the floor
at times. Perhaps along the empty halls

their skirts of taffeta, their woven shawls
left patterns—waves against a vanished shore—
linking the silences. Within these walls

they may have peered ahead, as through a caul,
and sensed, with those to come, a strange rapport.
At times, perhaps along the empty halls,

they stood to watch the snow, and saw it fall
in its endless way, blanketing the moors,
linking the silences. Within these walls

they blew the candle out, and slept. And all
was still around them now, and as before?
At times, perhaps—along the empty halls
linking the silences within these walls.

Berceuse

Step down into that darkness now, that dream
of drifting unremembrance and release,
where words and music form an endless stream

of syllables that swirl away and gleam
upon the flow, then vanish without cease.
Step down into that darkness: now that dream—

that fragment wave which in one moment seems
to break—returns, and on the next increase,
where words and music form an endless stream,

floods all resistance, all that would deem
mere waking marvelous, or knowledge peace.
Step down; into that darkness now, that dream,

descend, not to renounce but to redeem
the surface world. Within the water's lease,
where words and music form an endless stream,

letters appear in lines that have no theme
or purpose, yet their passing brings surcease.
Step down into that darkness now, that dream
where words and music form an endless stream.

Solstice

Awakened by the cries of distant crows,
he stares into the dark. Somewhere the light,
softened by drifts of newly fallen snow,

has gone astray: somehow the creatures know,
and call for its return. A kindred fright,
awakened by the cries of distant crows,

comes over him—that nothing more will grow,
lost in the cold and unregenerate night.
Softened by drifts of newly fallen snow,

the wind can barely gather strength to flow
along the garden path. Shrouded in white,
awakened by the cries of distant crows,

a single branch springs up, and throws off slow,
metallic flakes that seem to freeze in flight.
Softened by drifts of newly fallen snow,

they float within the first few rays to show
between the trees, then disappear from sight—
awakened by the cries of distant crows,
softened by drifts of newly fallen snow.

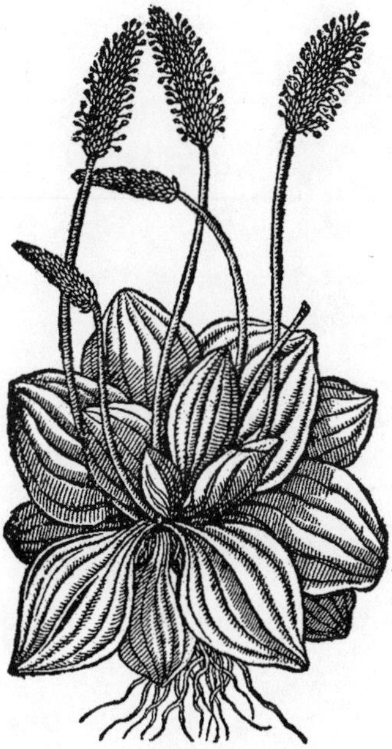

Bridge

We walk among the shadows: hand-hewn beams
beneath our feet begin to creak and splay.
Flower and branch above the flowing stream

abrade the shingles, dusty clapboards gleam
with scattered chinks. Reaching to feel our way,
we walk among the shadows. Hand-hewn beams

unlimber toward a central point that seems
to disappear in darkness, yet has stayed—
flower and branch above the flowing stream—

more than a century now. The rafters teem
with bits of nest and streaks of broken clay.
We walk among the shadows: hand-hewn beams

surround a square of light that will redeem
this narrow path, except for those who stray—
flower and branch above the flowing stream—

back toward that slow concurrence of extremes
where interlocking timbers still hold sway.
We walk among the shadows. Hand-hewn beams
flower and branch above the flowing stream.

Ditchweed

In the forgotten places where it still grows,
they come with green trash bags and gunnysacks.
No one ever sees anything, no one knows

what happens here. They walk down endless rows
of soybeans, out along the railroad tracks,
in the forgotten places. Where it still grows,

the banks own everything now. From windows
in the old farmhouses, no one glances back,
no one ever sees anything. No one knows

who drew the penciled map, or if it shows
the right way. Near woodpiles and hayracks,
in the forgotten places where it still grows,

wagons rust in the tall grass. Nobody mows
the weeds along these roads, or tars the cracks.
No one ever sees anything, no one knows

whose car is parked beside the bridge. SLOW
is the only sign the hunters leave intact
in the forgotten places. Where it still grows,
no one ever sees anything, no one knows.

Cemetery

Broken tombstones, paper flags—one sways,
held by a thread. Wind in the cedar trees.
Two blacksnakes come together in the maze

of shifting light—a momentary haze
of darkness shows among the jimson weeds,
broken tombstones, paper flags. One sways,

rests on a ledge, holding a level gaze;
the other waits—poised—tasting the breeze.
Two blacksnakes come together. In the maze

of sun and shadow, shot with beveled rays,
they drift among the green interstices,
broken tombstones, paper flags. One sways,

the other flows around it, sending waves
of permutation through the random leaves.
Two blacksnakes come together. In the maze

behind them, down the narrow passageways,
the grass unbends, the dimpled spider weaves.
Broken tombstones, paper flags—one sways.
Two blacksnakes come together in the maze.

Buzzards

Searching for balance in the endless flow
of wind above the ridge, they sail away,
striving to be still. In silence, to know

the hills, the road, the limestone creek below
the patchwork fields—to spend all day
searching for balance in the endless flow

of glancing thermals—unswerving shadows,
they spread their wings, managing to stay,
striving to be still. In silence to know—

watching to see which creatures far below
trudge on, and which have lost their way,
searching for balance in the endless flow—

they circle one more time, and come in low,
not far beyond a half-mown field of hay,
striving to be still. In silence, to know

is to walk across the stubble, past rows
of raked clover, and come to a quiet place—
searching for balance in the endless flow,
striving to be still. In silence, to know.

Portage

Vestigial signs remain. Marks in the rock —
a path between two unconnected streams —
still show the way, if you know where to look

and search for patterns lost beneath the cloak
of moss and lichen. Weathered notches gleam,
vestigial signs remain. Marks in the rock

tell when to go ashore, how long the trek
will take. Not far ahead, beech and hornbeam
still show the way, if you know where to look

among directions blazed against the bark;
healed over now, no longer scar but seam,
vestigial signs remain. Marks in the rock

stand out, discovered for a moment, struck
by the late-morning light. Forgotten schemes
still show the way, if you know where to look

within this dim, dissolving path, this book
of emblems opened to the wind, this dream.
Vestigial signs remain. Marks in the rock
still show the way, if you know where to look.

Plantain

Now they are calling—these ambient grasses
sprung up by the trail, asking if we remember
times when we lay down in windless places

sheltered from the glare, in noonday spaces
carved out by cicadas. With that same timbre,
now they are calling. These ambient grasses

leave footprints to follow, forgotten traces
of our walks together through the high timber,
times when we lay down. In windless places

we would wander, pausing to see our faces
among the rock pools, where no leaves tremble.
Now they are calling, these ambient grasses,

saying their names again among the mazes
of vagrant light, moments suspended in amber,
times when we lay down in windless places.

What the earth learned of those lost embraces,
what we knew there, pressed against it, lingers.
Now they are calling—these ambient grasses,
times when we lay down in windless places.

Interlude

Here is the spring I promised we would find
if we came back this way—a hollow space
beneath the hillside, waiting all this time

for us to angle through the leaves, and climb
down to the ledge, to where it slows its pace.
Here is the spring I promised we would find,

with elderberry blossoming, and thyme
and saxifrage along the limestone face.
Beneath the hillside, waiting all this time,

the falls, in overflowing steps, combine
to form an unexpected stopping-place.
Here is the spring I promised we would find:

across the pool, the accidental lines
and endless circles merge—a constant grace
beneath the hillside, waiting. All this time

has brought us here—to listen to the pines,
to drink, to watch the water striders race.
Here is the spring I promised we would find
beneath the hillside, waiting all this time.

Ford

A place of crossing over, where the river
starts its turn—a drift of glacial rocks
reveals a path, within the current's shadow,

to the other side. Here, streams of minnows
slip through the shallows, as if to mark
a place of crossing. Over where the river

broods, near the far bank, a fallen cedar,
bleached and smooth, stripped of its bark,
reveals a path. Within the current's shadow,

up close, the rocks have no special order;
you must choose, with each step you take,
a place of crossing over. Where the river

tangles and snarls but fails to scatter
the stones—that fracture, that break,
reveals a path within. The current's shadow

overwhelms you, there's no sign to follow,
no pattern now—your own momentum makes
a place of crossing over, where the river
reveals a path within the current's shadow.

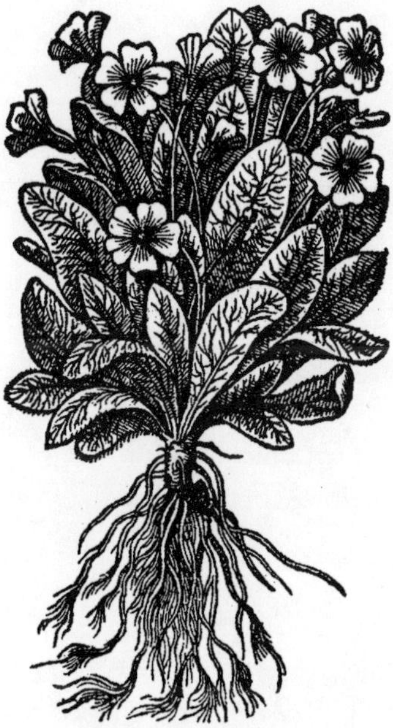

Millefiori

In the last glimmer of late afternoon,
burnished by the sun's oblique farewell,
a mirror shines, across an empty room,

a shimmering patch of light. A subtle fume
of brightness creeps along the dusty shelves
in the last glimmer of late afternoon;

immersed in shadow, rows of books are strewn
with dazzling motes. Like circles in a well,
a mirror shines across an empty room,

reaching from pen to letter knife, to spoon
and cup—as though reflection might dispel,
in the last glimmer of late afternoon,

oncoming night. Unhurried, like the moon's
ascent, or honey tipped from gleaming cells,
a mirror shines across an empty room,

a paperweight of myriad flowers blooms,
a softness flares within a whorled shell.
In the last glimmer of late afternoon
a mirror shines across an empty room.

Clavichord

Touch me once more, until these separate strands
begin to stir. My inarticulate keys
quicken beneath your soft, attentive hands,

my strings, responsive to your least commands,
give back strange overtones and harmonies.
Touch me once more. Until these separate strands

comply, and nothing hurried countermands
the way in which such gradual urgencies
quicken beneath your soft, attentive hands,

there can be no release—nor sarabandes
of meaning—in these plangent melodies.
Touch me once more, until these separate strands

commingle, and a newfound world expands
between us in this little room. Let seas
quicken beneath your soft, attentive hands,

let continents appear: who understands
this music loosens vast geographies.
Touch me once more, until these separate strands
quicken beneath your soft, attentive hands.

Waterspout

Filled with an errant, unavailing wind,
it walks on water. Impossibly serene,
rising through clear sky, burning within,

it stands—a shaft of holy fire gone dim
with disbelief, transmuted now, marine.
Filled with an errant, unavailing wind

it takes a serpent's shape, becomes a fin,
a cloud of tentacles, a troubled dream.
Rising through clear sky, burning within,

whirling—until its high, concentric spin
dissolves, and topples in a glassy sheen.
Filled with an errant, unavailing wind,

it scatters in a drifting spray—a scrim
through which a solitary gull is seen,
rising through clear sky. Burning within

the calm of sun and sea, poised to begin,
another spiral climbs the space between,
filled with an errant, unavailing wind,
rising through clear sky, burning within.

Loess

So far above us now, mimosa lifting,
reaching out to the rain's sporadic touch—
sheer walls of rock, a gray mist drifting,

obscuring long-needled branches, sifting
through intertangled roots. The view abrupt,
so far above us now—mimosa lifting

against the wrack, the pool, the shifting
stream of wind-blown waterfall that cuts
sheer walls of rock. A gray mist drifting,

issuing from sticks of incense, riffling
a scroll unraveling against the dusk,
so far above us now. Mimosa lifting

beyond the shadows, a pathway twisting
toward the heights, vanishing among hushed,
sheer walls of rock. A gray mist, drifting

along the paper's edge—a hand, risking
everything with each stroke of the brush.
So far above us now, mimosa lifting,
sheer walls of rock, a gray mist drifting.

Parfumeur

Set free among the rosewood-paneled rooms
on Royal Street, where mirrors line the walls,
the traces of a hundred choice perfumes

drift like forgotten voices from those tombs
untended now. Their soft, elusive calls,
set free among the rosewood-paneled rooms,

evoke a preternatural calm. Like plumes
of dust or smoke that momentarily stall,
the traces of a hundred choice perfumes

embody nothing, yet still serve to groom
the living, and to lend disguise. A pall,
set free among the rosewood-paneled rooms,

comes over our reflections in the gloom
of mirrored light. What further dusk befalls
the traces of a hundred choice perfumes

that swirl around us now? And what costumes,
what masks, are gathered here? What subtle flaws
set free, among the rosewood-paneled rooms,
the traces of a hundred choice perfumes?

Mandragora

Better to say the evening light's unraveling
now—that clouds threaten to shift and change;
better to call it merely darkness gathering

beyond the ridge. The wanderer, journeying
along the path, seeks refuge at the grange.
Better to say the evening light's unraveling:

where two roads cross, the sound of hammering
reverberates, then passes out of range.
Better to call it merely darkness gathering,

not shadows cast by the narrow scaffolding,
not shapes that dance in the lengths of chain.
Better to say the evening light's unraveling

where rain breaks through. The first drops, clattering
across the planks, dissolve against the grain.
Better to call it merely darkness gathering,

or a gust of wind that stirs the scattering
of flowers beneath the steps; nothing strange.
Better to say the evening light's unraveling,
better to call it merely darkness gathering.

Tankroom

Come together at last, no longer strangers,
braceleted with numbers, stripped of names,
asleep and drifting in these still waters,

they share a timeless urge—to be forever
lost in each other's arms, having no shame,
come together at last. No longer strangers,

they touch in casual ways we half remember—
moored in the twilight, tethered by a chain,
asleep and drifting. In these still waters

they dream of the moment when their fetters
will be struck off. Released from all blame,
come together at last, no longer strangers,

they will find their way. Now they encounter
only darkness enfolding, and endless rain.
Asleep and drifting in these still waters,

they must be born again, as broken embers
carried on the wind, or fragments of flame
come together at last—no longer strangers
asleep and drifting in these still waters.

Phosphorescence

What passed between us once was but a dream
that cast no shadow on the world of things.
Think of me now, in these dark days, as flame

that in a scattering of cubes still seems
to rise up from the vanished tree's lost rings.
What passed between us once was but a dream,

a slow and inverse fire that fell like rain
and shook the ashes from its brooding wings.
Think of me now, in these dark days, as flame

that burns in some unearthly way, like green
and silver branches dense with blossoming.
What passed between us once was but a dream,

a glimpse of loosened raiment, partially seen,
that falls away, and yet in falling, clings.
Think of me now, in these dark days, as flame

that with a colder, lasting light redeems
whatever loss such bright remembrance brings.
What passed between us once was but a dream.
Think of me now, in these dark days, as flame.

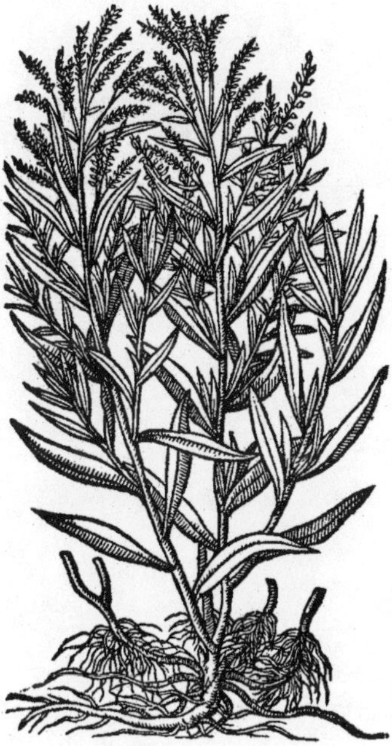

Palimpsest

The walk that led out through the apple trees—
the narrow, crumbling path of brick embossed
among the clumps of grass, the scattered leaves—

has vanished now. Each spring the peonies
come back, to drape their heavy bolls across
the walk that led out through the apple trees,

as if to show the way—until the breeze
dismantles them, and petals drift and toss
among the clumps of grass. The scattered leaves

half fill a plaited basket left to freeze
and thaw, and gradually darken into moss.
The walk that led out through the apple trees

has disappeared—unless, down on your knees,
searching beneath the vines that twist and cross
among the clumps of grass, the scattered leaves,

you scrape, and find—simplest of mysteries,
forgotten all this time, but not quite lost—
the walk that led out through the apple trees
among the clumps of grass, the scattered leaves.

Labyrinth

Somewhere, within the murmuring of things
that make no difference—aimlessly playing,
drifting in the wind—a loose door swings,

banging against a wall; the piece of string
that held it shut has blown away. Delaying,
somewhere within the murmuring of things,

crickets and tree toads pause, listening;
now they go on with their shrill surveying.
Drifting in the wind, a loose door swings

in widening arcs. Each rusty iron hinge
creaks in a different key: each is decaying,
somewhere within. The murmuring of things

wells up—the quickening thrum of wings,
the pulsing, intersecting voices swaying,
drifting in the wind. A loose door swings;

no torch, no adventitious thread brings
meaning to this maze, this endless straying
somewhere within the murmuring of things.
Drifting in the wind, a loose door swings.

Raincrow

Lost in the evening shadows now, you breathe
your strange sorrow—a pale lamp gleaming,
softly reclaimed again, among the leaves—

echo of long-forgotten hallways, wreathed
with faint perfume. I have heard you dreaming,
lost in the evening shadows. Now you breathe

upon the mirror, and their faces show beneath
the stairway. I stand beside them, beaming,
softly reclaimed again among the leaves.

What is it that you place before us, sheathed
in darkness? What fragrant beaker teeming,
lost in the evening shadows? Now you breathe

your five notes, and the wind's reply seethes
through the branches; the twilight, streaming
softly, reclaimed again among the leaves,

gathers around us, and your song bequeaths
approaching rain, and solitude, and seeming.
Lost in the evening shadows now you breathe,
softly reclaimed again among the leaves.

Linen

Scattered among bundles of flax in the rain,
pinned under water by smooth stones—broken,
spun, wound, and gathered in bright skeins

of blond thread, like bronze or silk—I gained
knowledge of the old ways long unspoken,
scattered among bundles of flax. In the rain

I was scutched to the marrow, yet no pain
could reach me—I had become that token
spun, wound, and gathered. In bright skeins

of filament, to be woven—to be changed
into pattern, as though having woken,
scattered among bundles of flax in the rain,

but risen up through darkness, newly arrayed
with morning. And would become, in time, omen
spun, wound, and gathered in bright skeins

of light, rags into paper, unconstrained
words cast there like silk, or bronze gnomon—
scattered among bundles of flax in the rain,
spun, wound, and gathered in bright skeins.

Sortilege

Where the phlox gleams, and the blue hydrangea,
sifted by the wind, leaves streaked with rain,
rises and falls, and yet nothing changes

along the gravel walks—there's no danger,
the thunder's muffled now, the lightning wanes
where the phlox gleams, and the blue hydrangea

turns in its stillness toward the far ranges
of evening. A layer of mist, unexplained,
rises and falls. And yet nothing changes,

I hear your step along the path—no stranger
to these branching ways, this terminal moraine
where the phlox gleams, and the blue hydrangea

drifts in the shadows. The night wind deranges
the vines around the western gate, strains,
rises and falls, and yet nothing changes;

the rustle of leaves softens and rearranges
the sound of your voice in these last refrains,
where the phlox gleams, and the blue hydrangea
rises and falls. And yet nothing changes.

Reprise

Only an evening wind that comes at last
before sleep falls—a distant beckoning
so long forgotten, out of dark rains past—

wind that the scent of water lilies, massed
and set adrift and softly gleaming, brings.
Only an evening wind, that comes at last

and carries memory with it, anchored fast
in the flow of things. Hushed imaginings,
so long forgotten, out of dark rains past,

or hands that rest now, in the aftermath
of music echoing deep within the strings.
Only an evening wind, that comes at last,

that has no shape or form, nor earthly task
except to draw up from those hidden springs
so long forgotten, out of dark rains past,

an elemental motion. Hearing, we ask,
and yet we know, beyond all reckoning—
only an evening wind that comes at last,
so long forgotten, out of dark rains past.

Hawkmoth

Freed of all cerements of sleep, unfurled
in shadow—touch me now with your wings'
imagined light, lift me toward your world

of vision, of dark flight. When I would curl
inchoate, show me these luminescent things
freed of all cerements of sleep. Unfurled,

I searched the labyrinth, but night hurled
me into nothingness; teach me to sing,
imagined light, lift me. Toward your world

tempt me along the winding path, whirled
by its dust, its storms, that I might spring—
freed of all cerements of sleep—unfurled

upon the naked day, and by some structural
fury or design, from out of darkness bring
imagined light. Lift me toward your world,

riddler, through all the chaos and the swirl,
find me out deeply with your soft sting,
freed of all cerements of sleep, unfurled.
Imagined light, lift me toward your world.

Comet

Somewhere not far beyond these barricades
mysterious, a single branch is burning.
To the dim light and the large circle of shade

I would return, and by green leaves arrayed
with broken fire, regain a different learning,
somewhere not far beyond. These barricades

are all instruction now, these sounds evade
the measure, and the swarm's impulsive churning.
To the dim light and the large circle of shade

I would be summoned—image shattered, made
again into a thousand shapes of yearning,
somewhere not far. Beyond these barricades

the scattered pieces come together, swayed
by spectral lines that draw the most discerning
to the dim light and the large circle of shade.

Along this path we cannot be conveyed
but move as particles or waves, returning—
somewhere not far, beyond these barricades—
to the dim light and the large circle of shade.

Notes

Book title: the composition for harpsichord, "Les Barricades Mystérieuses," by François Couperin (1668-1733), occurs sixth in Couperin's second book of *Ordres*, published in 1713. It is a resonant, polyphonic piece of some two minutes' duration. The title remains an enigma.

Cover illustration: after Edward Calvert's "Chamber Idyll," which first appeared in 1831. The original print, a wood engraving, measures 3 x 1.5 inches. Calvert (1799-1883) was one of a group of young English artists who gathered around William Blake in his old age.

Interior illustrations: after the original woodcuts in *The Herball or General Historie of Plantes* by John Gerard, published-in 1597, 1633, and 1636; and as shown in Dover's 1969 version, *Leaves from Gerard's Herball*, arranged by Marcus Woodward. The prints reproduced here are "Medow-Grasse" (page ix), "Plantaine" (page 9), "Field Primrose" (page 19), "Tarragon" (page 29), and "Bright Wheat" (back cover).

Epigraph, page vii: from Blake's *A Descriptive Catalogue*, prepared for an exhibition of sixteen of his watercolors and drawings in London in 1809.

Encore, page 6: still, again.

Berceuse, page 7: lullaby or falling-asleep song.

Ditchweed, page 12: American slang term for the hemp plant when found in a wild, uncultivated state.

Plantain, page 16: a short, broad-leaved plant found in lawns, fields, and waste places. Most often regarded as a weed, it was known to the Romans as a remedy for cuts and abrasions. Both Chaucer and Shakespeare refer to its curative powers. Common plantain, illustrated on page 9, is widely distributed.

Millefiori, page 21: or "thousand flowers," a type of ornamental glass made by cutting cross sections of fused bundles of glass rods of various colors and sizes.

Clavichord, page 22: an early keyboard instrument. Its responsive "touch" communicating between finger, key, and inner mechanism enables the player to achieve subtle modifications in vibrato and pitch. According to Kathleen Schlesinger, in the eleventh edition of the *Encyclopaedia Britannica,* "the tone of the clavichord, extremely sweet and delicate, was characterized by a tremulous hesitancy, which formed its great charm while rendering it suitable only for the private music room or study."

"sarabande," page 22, line 10: a dance, said to be derived originally from the Saracens, which first appeared in Spain in the sixteenth century. In Europe during the following two centuries it evolved into a stately court dance resembling the minuet. The music for the sarabande is in slow triple time.

Loess, page 24: aeolian or windblown rock. In geology a variety of soft, porous rock that is yellowish or buff in color. Its most remarkable property is its capacity to retain vertical walls, or even overhanging ledges, along the banks of streams and rivers.

Parfumeur, page 25: Hové Parfumeur, Ltd., founded in 1931, is the oldest perfume manufacturer in New Orleans. From its showrooms on Royal Street, in the French Quarter, it is a short walk to Rampart Street and the Saint Louis Cemetery No. 1, established in 1789.

Mandragora, page 26: the mandrake plant, known in classical times for its ability to relieve pain in surgery and childbirth. In Europe during the late middle ages the superstition arose that a mandrake root was most potent when found under a gallows, and that such plants grew from the congealed urine and semen which drops from a hanged man.

Tankroom, page 27: unofficial term for a restricted area in a medical school or teaching hospital containing one or more large receptacles in which human cadavers intended for anatomical study are temporarily stored.

Phosphorescence, page 28: in this instance, fox fire, a pale, silvery light issuing from scattered fragments of a decayed stump or log that has been taken over by a form of bioluminescence.

Raincrow, page 33: in parts of the American Middle West, a folk term for the mourning dove.

Sortilege, page 35: sorcery.

"terminal moraine," page 35, line 11: a long, sinuous hill consisting of earth, rock, and stones deposited by a retreating glacier.

Villanelle: a verse form which has its earliest origins in Italian folk song and in the circular patterns of the rustic dance. At the beginning of the seventeenth century poets in France experimented with variations which contributed to the villanelle's evolution. After a long dormancy, it was revived in the mid-nineteenth century — principally by French poets — and given its present form. *Villanelle* may be traced back through the Italian *villanella* to *villano,* a peasant or farm hand, which in turn derives from the Latin *villa,* a farm house or house in the country.

Acknowledgments

Improvisation	*Poetry*
Dusk	*The Formalist*
Summons	*The Laurel Review*
Riverdrift	*The Lyric*
Candle	*The Formalist*
Encore	*The Review*
Berceuse	*The Formalist*
Solstice	*The Long Story*
Bridge	*Tumcumcari Literary Review*
Ditchweed	*Outposts Poetry Quarterly*
Cemetery	*Outposts Poetry Quarterly*
Buzzards	*Hellas*
Portage	*Snowy Egret*
Plantain	*South Carolina Review*
Interlude	*Free Lunch*
Ford	*South Carolina Review*
Millefiori	*The Long Story*
Clavichord	*Curriculum Vitae*
Waterspout	*The Laurel Review*
Loess	*The Lyric*
Parfumeur	*The Laurel Review*
Mandragora	*Defined Providence*
Tankroom	*Mockingbird*
Phosphorescence	*The Iowa Review*
Palimpsest	*Sou'wester*
Labyrinth	*The Formalist*
Raincrow	*Yarrow*
Linen	*Poetry*
Sortilege	*The Dark Horse*
Reprise	*South Carolina Review*
Hawkmoth	*Poetry*
Comet	*Defined Providence*

About the Author

Jared Carter's first collection of poems, *Work, for the Night Is Coming*, won the Walt Whitman Award for 1980. His second, *After the Rain*, received the Poets' Prize for 1995.

He was a recipient of the Indiana Governor's Arts Award in 1985. His fellowships include grants from the National Endowment for the Arts and the John Simon Guggenheim Memorial Foundation.

His two collections, along with an earlier chapbook of poems, *Pincushion's Strawberry*, are available from the Cleveland State University Poetry Center.